I0416743

HOW TO BUDGET

AND CAREER PLANNING For Teens

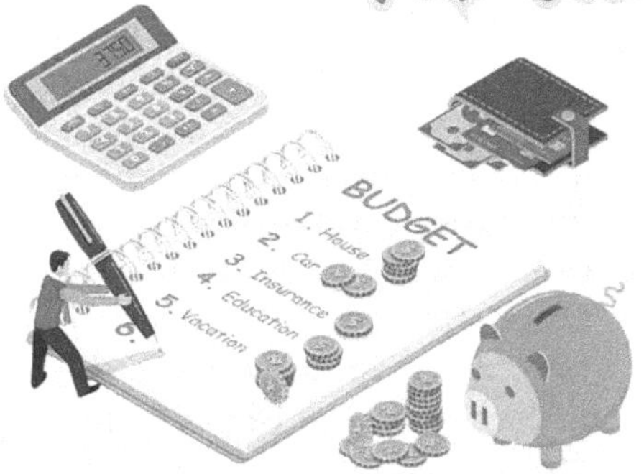
BUDGET
1. House
2. Car
3. Insurance
4. Education
5. Vacation
6.

Practical Tips for Teenagers to Thrive Financially

Heath Powers

For free consultation and assistance on How to Budget for teens feel free to contact me with questions or for more information.
Powerswealth555@gmail.com

Budgeting is telling your money where to go instead of wondering where it went." - John Maxwell

"A budget is more than just numbers on a page; it's a roadmap to your financial dreams"

ABOUT THE AUTHOR

Heath Powers is a seasoned financial advisor with over a decade of experience empowering individuals to take control of their finances. With a passion for educating young adults on the importance of financial literacy, Heath has dedicated his career to helping teens navigate the complexities of budgeting and money management. As a parent himself, Heath understands the challenges teenagers face when it comes to handling money responsibly and strives to provide practical guidance tailored to their unique needs.

Drawing from his extensive expertise in personal finance and his ability to communicate complex concepts in an accessible manner, Heath has crafted "How to Budget for Teens" as a comprehensive resource designed to equip young readers with the tools they need to make informed financial decisions and build a solid foundation for their future success. Through his engaging writing style and relatable anecdotes, Heath empowers teens to take charge of their financial futures with confidence and clarity.

TABLE OF CONTENT

INTRODUCTION

Budgeting, in its essence, is a strategic plan that allocates one's financial resources, encompassing income and expenses, within a specified period. For teenagers, comprehending this practice is akin to obtaining a roadmap for their financial journey into adulthood. It's not merely about handling money; rather, it's a skill that empowers them to make informed decisions, manage resources effectively, and work toward their aspirations.

Understanding the basics of budgeting starts with recognizing the value it holds. Teens will learn that a budget is more than restricting spending; it's a tool that grants them control and freedom simultaneously. It allows them to prioritise their needs and wants while ensuring they're not derailed by impulsive spending. Through this understanding, they gain a sense of financial responsibility, crucial for their future independence.

The introduction focuses on the significance of early financial literacy. It emphasises that developing budgeting skills early on provides teens with a strong foundation for navigating the complexities of personal finance in adulthood. It encourages proactive financial behaviour, fostering a mindset where financial planning becomes a habit rather than a chore.

Moreover, the introduction highlights the broader context of budgeting, demonstrating its relevance beyond individual needs. It sheds light on how effective budgeting contributes to economic stability and resilience on a larger scale. By managing personal finances prudently, teens contribute to their own financial well-being and potentially the prosperity of their communities.This chapter aims to inspire teens by illustrating success stories of individuals who started budgeting early and reaped the benefits in their lives.

Real-life examples can motivate and show the practical advantages of implementing budgeting principles.The introduction to budgeting sets the tone for the entire book, emphasising the pivotal role budgeting plays in shaping a stable financial future. It encourages teens to embrace this learning journey, assuring them that with commitment and discipline, they can gain control of their finances, enabling them to achieve their dreams and aspirations.

CHAPTER 1

Understanding the basics

Understanding the basics of budgeting is pivotal for teenagers embarking on their journey toward financial independence. This section elucidates the fundamental principles and components that form the bedrock of effective budget management.At its core, budgeting revolves around comprehending two crucial elements: income and expenses. Income refers to the money received, typically through sources like part-time jobs, allowances, or other means available to teens.

Understanding income entails recognizing its variability, whether it's steady or irregular, and grasping the importance of accurately tracking it.Conversely, expenses encompass all the monetary outflows. This includes both needs—essential expenditures like food, clothing, and education—and wants, which encompass non-essential purchases such as entertainment or luxury items.This section aids teens in categorising their expenses, discerning between necessities and desires, thereby laying the groundwork for informed decision-making.

Creating a comprehensive overview of income and expenses forms the cornerstone of an effective budget. Teens learn the significance of creating a realistic, detailed budget that accounts for both fixed and variable expenses. This understanding enables them to allocate resources judiciously, ensuring that they have enough for essentials while still leaving room for discretionary spending.Moreover, this section introduces the concept of budgeting as a proactive tool rather than a restrictive measure.

Teens discover that a budget is not solely about curtailing spending but rather about directing it purposefully. It fosters a mindset shift, encouraging them to view budgeting as a means of aligning their spending habits with their financial goals, thereby empowering them to achieve their aspirations.In addition to income and expenses, understanding the concept of tracking and monitoring finances is crucial.

Introducing teens to various budgeting tools, such as spreadsheets or apps, equips them with the necessary resources to keep tabs on their financial inflows and outflows. By regularly tracking their finances, they gain insights into their spending patterns, enabling them to make informed adjustments as needed.Furthermore, this section touches upon the significance of flexibility within a budget.It elucidates that life is dynamic, and financial circumstances might change.

Teaching teens to embrace adaptability within their budgets helps them navigate unexpected expenses or changes in income, ensuring their financial plan remains robust and relevant.Understanding the basics of budgeting isn't solely about numbers; it's about fostering a holistic mindset shift toward responsible financial management.

This chapter aims to imbue teens with the knowledge that effective budgeting is a skillset that extends far beyond adolescence, serving as a lifelong tool for financial stability and empowerment. It lays the groundwork for subsequent chapters, setting the stage for deeper exploration into more intricate budgeting strategies and financial concepts.

Importance of budgeting for teens

Budgeting holds immense importance for teenagers as it lays the groundwork for responsible financial habits and a secure future. This section elaborates on the multifaceted significance of budgeting in the lives of adolescents.Firstly, budgeting instils financial discipline from an early age. It empowers teens to take charge of their money, teaching them to prioritise and allocate funds judiciously.

By understanding the value of money and the effort required to earn it, teens develop a sense of responsibility and accountability in managing their finances.Moreover, budgeting cultivates a sense of financial awareness and mindfulness. Teens learn to differentiate between needs and wants, understanding the impact of their spending choices. This awareness helps them make informed decisions, preventing impulsive purchases and fostering a habit of thoughtful spending, which is essential in an age of constant consumerism and advertising.

Budgeting also serves as a tool for goal-setting and achievement. Through budgeting, teenagers can outline their financial goals—whether it's saving for a specific purchase, funding education, or preparing for future endeavours. By breaking down these aspirations into actionable steps within their budget, they gain a clearer path toward realising their dreams.Additionally, budgeting imparts crucial life skills beyond managing money.

It teaches organisational skills, time management, and problem-solving, as teens navigate through allocating resources effectively while balancing their expenses and savings. These skills are transferable and beneficial in various aspects of their lives, including academics and future careers.Furthermore, budgeting offers a safety net in times of financial uncertainty.

It prepares teens for unexpected situations or emergencies, allowing them to handle unforeseen expenses without compromising their financial stability. This sense of preparedness instils confidence and resilience, enabling teens to face challenges more effectively.Understanding the importance of budgeting also fosters open communication about finances within families. As teens grasp the significance of budgeting, it encourages discussions about money matters at home.

This transparency aids in building a strong foundation for financial literacy within the family unit, empowering teens to seek guidance and advice from parents or guardians.Moreover, effective budgeting in adolescence sets the stage for a financially responsible adulthood. Teens who grasp budgeting early are more likely to carry these skills into their future, making informed financial decisions as they transition into independent living, higher education, or entering the workforce.

Ultimately, the importance of budgeting for teens transcends mere financial management—it lays the groundwork for a lifetime of responsible decision-making, prudent spending, and achieving financial goals. It empowers them to navigate the complexities of the modern financial world with confidence, setting them on a path toward financial independence and success.

CHAPTER 2

Setting Financial Goals

Setting financial goals is a fundamental aspect of effective budgeting for teenagers, providing direction and purpose to their financial planning. This section focuses on the significance of goal-setting and the steps involved in establishing and pursuing these objectives.Financial goals act as guiding stars, offering a clear vision of what teens want to achieve with their money. These goals can range from short-term objectives, like saving for a new gadget, to long-term ambitions such as funding higher education or purchasing a car.

By defining these goals, teens gain a sense of purpose and motivation, driving their financial decisions and actions.The process of setting financial goals begins with introspection and reflection. Teens are encouraged to envision their aspirations, determining what they desire to accomplish financially in the short, medium, and long term. Encouraging them to dream big while maintaining a sense of practicality helps in crafting realistic and achievable goals.Once these goals are established, the next step involves quantifying and detailing them.

Teens learn the importance of setting specific, measurable, achievable, relevant, and time-bound (SMART) goals. For instance, instead of a vague goal like "save money," a SMART goal would be "save $500 in six months to purchase a laptop for college."Additionally, this section emphasises the importance of prioritising goals. Teens might have several aspirations, but not all can be pursued simultaneously.Understanding the hierarchy of goals helps in determining which ones to focus on first.

This process involves evaluating the urgency, importance, and feasibility of each goal within the context of their overall financial situation.Teens are encouraged to break down larger, long-term goals into smaller, manageable milestones. This approach makes the goals less overwhelming and allows for incremental progress. It also enables them to track their advancement and celebrate achievements along the way, fostering a sense of accomplishment and motivation.

Moreover, this section highlights the need for flexibility in goal-setting. Life is dynamic, and circumstances might change. Encouraging teens to review and reassess their goals periodically allows them to adapt to changes in their lives, ensuring that their financial objectives remain relevant and realistic.Setting financial goals isn't solely about monetary targets; it also encompasses personal growth and development. Teens learn that financial goals are intertwined with their values and aspirations.

Achieving these goals isn't just about the destination; it's also about the journey, the lessons learned, and the skills acquired along the way.Ultimately, setting financial goals for teens is a transformative process. It helps them envision their future, instil a sense of purpose, and cultivates a habit of disciplined financial planning. By embracing goal-setting as an integral part of budgeting, teenagers lay a solid foundation for a financially secure and fulfilling life ahead.

Identifying short and long-term goals

Identifying short and long-term financial goals is a cornerstone of effective budgeting for teens, allowing them to chart a clear path towards their aspirations while developing a comprehensive financial plan.Short-term goals typically encompass objectives achievable within a shorter timeframe, usually spanning a few weeks to a year. These might include saving for a specific purchase, like a new phone or a trip, or covering immediate expenses such as extracurricular activities or hobbies.

Identifying short-term goals allows teenagers to experience the satisfaction of accomplishment more quickly, fostering a sense of motivation and progress in their financial journey.Conversely, long-term goals extend beyond immediate gratification, encompassing aspirations that span several years or even decades. These could involve saving for higher education, purchasing a car, or building a solid emergency fund.

Identifying long-term goals requires a broader perspective and often involves more strategic planning, incorporating incremental steps towards achieving larger milestones.When teaching teens to identify short and long-term goals, it's crucial to emphasise the importance of specificity and clarity. Short-term goals benefit from being more concrete and immediate, while long-term goals may require more detailed planning and periodic reassessment.

Encouraging teens to define their objectives in measurable terms helps them track progress and stay motivated.Short-term goals are like stepping stones toward long-term aspirations. They offer teens a sense of achievement and momentum, acting as building blocks for their larger financial objectives. By focusing on and accomplishing short-term goals, teens learn the value of consistent effort and perseverance, essential qualities in achieving their broader, more ambitious long-term aims.

Moreover, the identification of short and long-term goals aids in prioritisation. Teens might have multiple goals, but understanding which ones are urgent and which are more distant helps in allocating resources accordingly. This process enables them to create a hierarchy of goals, ensuring that they're directing their efforts towards what matters most at any given time.Additionally, identifying these goals encourages forward-thinking and strategic planning.

Teens develop the foresight to anticipate future needs and prepare for them accordingly. Long-term goals necessitate proactive planning, encouraging teens to think about their future financial security and the steps needed to achieve it.Furthermore, it's crucial to highlight that goals aren't set in stone. Circumstances change, and so do priorities.

Encouraging flexibility and periodic reassessment allows teens to adapt their goals as their lives evolve, ensuring that their financial plan remains relevant and achievable.In essence, identifying short and long-term financial goals equips teenagers with the foresight, discipline, and direction needed to navigate their financial future. By understanding the distinction between short and long-term objectives and embracing them as integral parts of their budgeting journey, teens set themselves on a path towards financial responsibility and success.

Creating a Roadmap to Achieve them

Creating a roadmap to achieve financial goals is a pivotal step for teenagers, providing a structured and actionable plan that translates their aspirations into reality. This section focuses on the strategic approach required to attain these goals, emphasising the importance of planning, organisation, and consistency.The process of crafting a roadmap begins by breaking down each financial goal into smaller, manageable steps.

For instance, if the goal is to save a certain amount for a summer trip, the roadmap might involve calculating how much needs to be saved each month and identifying areas where expenses can be minimised to allocate more funds toward the goal.Moreover, the roadmap involves setting timelines and deadlines. By establishing specific timeframes for achieving different milestones, teenagers create a sense of urgency and accountability.

This temporal structure aids in maintaining focus and ensuring steady progress towards their financial objectives.The roadmap also entails identifying potential obstacles and devising strategies to overcome them. Teenagers learn to anticipate challenges that might hinder their progress and proactively plan for contingencies. This might involve finding additional sources of income, cutting down on certain expenses, or seeking support and advice from parents or mentors.

Furthermore, this section emphasises the significance of leveraging tools and resources to assist in achieving these goals.

It could involve utilising budgeting apps, spreadsheets, or setting up automatic transfers to savings accounts. These tools aid in tracking progress, staying organised, and ensuring adherence to the established roadmap.In addition to tools, fostering a habit of consistency and discipline is essential.

Teens learn that consistent effort, even if incremental, contributes significantly to reaching their goals. Consistency instils a sense of commitment and responsibility, laying the groundwork for successful goal attainment.The roadmap also incorporates the importance of periodic reviews and adjustments. Life is dynamic, and circumstances change. Encouraging teens to assess their progress regularly allows them to make necessary adjustments to their roadmap.

It's an opportunity to celebrate achievements, recalibrate goals if needed, and stay aligned with their overall financial plan.Moreover, encouraging teens to seek guidance and support from trusted sources is crucial. Whether it's seeking advice from parents, teachers, or financial advisors, having a support system aids in staying accountable and motivated throughout the journey.Lastly, instilling a sense of patience and perseverance is key. Achieving financial goals often requires time and persistence.

Teens learn that setbacks are part of the process, and maintaining a positive attitude while staying committed to their roadmap is essential in overcoming challenges.In essence, creating a roadmap to achieve financial goals empowers teenagers with a structured plan of action. By breaking down their aspirations into manageable steps, setting timelines, leveraging tools, and maintaining consistency, teens gain the skills and mindset needed to navigate their financial journey successfully. This roadmap serves as a guiding light, leading them towards realising their dreams while instilling valuable life lessons of discipline, adaptability, and determination.

CHAPTER 3

Creating Your Budget

Creating a budget is a foundational skill for teenagers, offering them a framework to manage their finances effectively. This process involves understanding income, categorising expenses, and utilising tools to develop a comprehensive financial plan tailored to their needs and aspirations.

Understanding Income:

The first step in creating a budget is comprehending income sources. For teenagers, this may include earnings from part-time jobs, allowances, or monetary gifts. It's crucial to identify the regularity and stability of income streams, distinguishing between fixed and variable sources.

Categorising Expenses:

Categorising expenses is equally pivotal. Expenses typically fall into two main categories: needs and wants. Needs encompass essential expenditures like food, clothing, education-related costs, and transportation. Wants encompass discretionary spending on entertainment, hobbies, or non-essential items.

Income Minus Expenses:

The core principle of budgeting lies in ensuring that total income exceeds total expenses. This entails subtracting total expenses from total income to determine whether there's a surplus or deficit. For teenagers, this surplus could be allocated to savings, investments, or additional discretionary spending, while a deficit signals the need to adjust spending habits or find ways to increase income.

Budgeting Tools:

Utilising budgeting tools simplifies the process and aids in maintaining financial records. Teens can opt for various tools like spreadsheets, mobile apps, or specialised budgeting software. These tools streamline budget creation, expense tracking, and goal monitoring, offering real-time insights into their financial situation.

Allocating Funds:

Once income and expenses are identified, allocating funds becomes crucial. This involves assigning specific amounts to various expense categories while ensuring that essential needs are prioritised. Creating spending limits for discretionary categories fosters disciplined spending habits.

Emergency Fund And Savings:

Encouraging teens to allocate a portion of their income to an emergency fund and savings is essential. The emergency fund acts as a safety net for unforeseen expenses, while savings contribute towards achieving short and long-term financial goals, instilling a habit of financial preparedness.

Monitoring And Adjusting:

Regularly monitoring the budget's performance is vital. Teens should review their budget periodically, comparing actual spending against the budgeted amounts. This analysis helps identify areas where adjustments might be necessary, ensuring the budget remains realistic and aligned with their financial goals.

Adaptability And Flexibility:

Budgets aren't static; they require adaptability and flexibility. Encouraging teens to embrace changes in income or expenses and adjust their budget accordingly fosters resilience and proactive financial management.

Financial Goals Alignment:

Aligning the budget with financial goals is a critical aspect. Teens should integrate their savings and spending habits into the budget to ensure they're progressing towards their aspirations.

Communication And Accountability:

Promoting open communication about budgeting within families cultivates a supportive environment. Accountability and guidance from parents or mentors aid teenagers in staying committed to their budgeting goals.

Developing Financial Discipline:

Creating and adhering to a budget instils financial discipline. It teaches teenagers to prioritise spending, differentiate between needs and wants, and make informed financial decisions.

Building A Lifelong Skill:

Lastly, emphasising that budgeting is a lifelong skill is crucial. It's a tool that teenagers will carry into adulthood, enabling them to navigate financial complexities confidently.

Creating a budget involves understanding income, categorising expenses, utilising tools, allocating funds, establishing emergency funds and savings, monitoring, adapting, aligning with financial goals, fostering communication, developing discipline, and recognizing the lifelong value of budgeting. It's a fundamental skill that empowers teenagers to manage their finances responsibly and shape a secure financial future.

Income vs. expenses: knowing the difference

Understanding the difference between income and expenses forms the bedrock of effective budgeting, empowering teenagers to manage their finances prudently. This comprehension involves recognizing the sources of income and categorising various types of expenses to establish a balanced financial framework.

Income:

Income refers to the money received by individuals through various channels. For teenagers, income sources primarily include earnings from part-time jobs, allowances from parents, monetary gifts, or any other means of financial inflow. It's essential to distinguish between different forms of income, whether they are fixed, regular, or irregular.

Fixed income comprises consistent sources of money, such as a monthly allowance or a set paycheck from a part-time job. Understanding the reliability of fixed income aids in predicting available funds for budgeting purposes. In contrast, irregular income, like monetary gifts or sporadic earnings, presents challenges in consistent budget planning, requiring flexibility and contingency plans.

Expenses:
Expenses encompass the various outflows of money incurred to cover needs and wants. Categorising expenses into essential needs and

discretionary wants helps teenagers discern the significance of different expenditures.

Needs:

Needs constitute essential expenses crucial for daily living. These include expenditures on food, housing, utilities, education-related costs, transportation, and healthcare. Needs are non-negotiable expenses vital for sustaining a healthy and functional lifestyle. Teaching teenagers to prioritise needs ensures that essential expenses are covered before discretionary spending.

Wants:

Wants encompass discretionary expenses that aren't necessary for survival but contribute to personal enjoyment and fulfilment. These expenses may involve entertainment, dining out, hobbies, fashion, or non-essential gadgets. Distinguishing between needs and wants aids teenagers in making conscious spending decisions, allocating resources sensibly, and avoiding impulsive purchases.

Balancing Income And Expenses:

Understanding the relationship between income and expenses is pivotal. Budgeting involves ensuring that total income exceeds total expenses, resulting in a surplus. This surplus can then be directed towards savings, investments, or additional discretionary spending.In cases where expenses surpass income, a deficit occurs, necessitating adjustments in spending habits or finding avenues to increase income.

This awareness highlights the importance of aligning expenses with income, encouraging teenagers to live within their means and avoid accruing debt.Teaching the difference between income and expenses instils financial responsibility, prudent decision-making, and foresight. It equips teenagers with the foundational knowledge needed to create a balanced budget, allocate funds efficiently, and cultivate lifelong habits of responsible financial management.

Comprehending income and expenses involves identifying sources of income, categorising needs versus wants in expenditures, ensuring a surplus between income and expenses, and making informed decisions to live within one's means. This understanding forms the basis for sound budgeting practices, enabling teenagers to navigate their finances with prudence and foresight.

Budgeting Tools and Techniques For Teens

Budgeting tools and techniques play a crucial role in aiding teens to manage their finances effectively. These tools empower teenagers to track their income, categorise expenses, set financial goals, and make informed decisions.

Here's an exploration of various budgeting tools and techniques suitable for teens:

1. Spreadsheet Software:

Using spreadsheet software like Microsoft Excel or Google Sheets offers a customizable and versatile platform for budgeting. Teens can create their budget templates, input income sources, categorise expenses, and track spending. It provides a visual representation of their financial situation, facilitating easy adjustments and analysis.

2. Budgeting Apps:

There are numerous budgeting apps tailored for teens available on smartphones and tablets. Apps like Mint, YNAB (You Need a Budget), or PocketGuard allow teens to sync their bank accounts, set spending limits, track expenses in real-time, and receive alerts when nearing budget limits. The user-friendly interface and accessibility make these apps an attractive option for teach-ins by teenagers.

3. Envelope System:

The envelope system involves allocating cash into labelled envelopes for various spending categories, such as groceries, entertainment, or transportation. This tactile method allows teens to physically see and manage their spending, promoting conscious decision-making and preventing overspending in specific categories.

4. Online Budgeting Tools:

Online budgeting tools offer interactive platforms for teens to manage their finances. Websites like BudgetSimple, EveryDollar, or Personal Capital provide budgeting templates, expense tracking, and goal-setting features. These tools offer convenience and accessibility for teenagers who prefer online interfaces over traditional methods.

5. Automated Savings Apps:

Certain apps specialise in automating savings for specific goals. For instance, apps like Acorns or Qapital round up purchases to the nearest dollar and allocate the spare change into a savings account or investment portfolio. This method encourages consistent savings without requiring manual effort.

6. Zero-Based Budgeting:

Zero-based budgeting involves allocating every dollar of income to various expense categories or savings, ensuring that the total income minus expenses equals zero. This method promotes thorough planning and accountability, encouraging teens to assign purpose to every dollar earned.

7. Visual Aids And Charts:

Visual aids like charts, graphs, or diagrams provide a clear overview of spending patterns and financial goals. Teens can create visual representations of their budgeting progress, making it easier to comprehend and stay motivated to adhere to their financial plan.

8. Cash Flow Forecasting:

Forecasting future income and expenses aids in long-term financial planning. Teens can anticipate major expenditures, irregular income, or seasonal changes, allowing for better preparation and allocation of resources.

Introducing and guiding teens on these budgeting tools and techniques instils financial literacy, fosters responsible spending habits, and cultivates a proactive approach to managing money. Encouraging experimentation with different tools helps them find the method that best suits their preferences and lifestyle, setting them on the path to financial independence and success.

CHAPTER 4

Smart Spending Habits

Smart spending habits are essential for teenagers, guiding them to make informed and responsible financial decisions. These habits enable teens to differentiate between needs and wants, prioritise spending, and maximise the value of their money. Here's an exploration of smart spending habits:

1.Differentiating Between Needs And Wants:

Understanding the difference between needs and wants forms the foundation of smart spending. Needs are essential for survival and well-being, such as food, shelter, education, and healthcare. Wants, on the other hand, are non-essential desires, like entertainment, luxury items, or unnecessary gadgets. Encouraging teens to prioritise needs helps them allocate resources sensibly and avoid unnecessary expenses.

2. Creating A Budget And Sticking To It:

Establishing and adhering to a budget fosters disciplined spending. Teens learn to allocate specific amounts to various expense categories, ensuring that they don't overspend. Sticking to a budget aids in avoiding impulsive purchases and encourages thoughtful spending aligned with their financial goals.

3. Comparison Shopping:

Encouraging teens to compare prices and explore various options before making a purchase is a valuable habit. This habit helps them find the best deals, discounts, or value-for-money options, ensuring they get the most out of their money without compromising quality.

4. Avoiding Impulse Purchases:

Impulse buying can lead to unnecessary expenses and derail budget plans. Teaching teens to pause and consider whether a purchase is necessary or aligns with their financial goals helps in avoiding impulsive decisions. Waiting before making a purchase allows time for reflection, reducing unnecessary spending.

5. Seeking Value Over Price:

Smart spending involves considering the long-term value of a purchase rather than solely focusing on the price. Encouraging teens to assess the quality, durability, and usefulness of an item helps them make purchases that offer lasting value, even if they might have a higher upfront cost.

6. Practising Delayed Gratification:

Cultivating the habit of delayed gratification helps teenagers in managing their finances. Understanding that delaying certain purchases or saving towards a goal can lead to more significant rewards in the future instils patience and discipline in spending.

7. Avoiding Debt and Credit Misuse:

Teaching teens about the pitfalls of debt and the responsible use of credit cards is crucial. Understanding that debt accrues interest and can lead to financial stress helps in cultivating a habit of avoiding unnecessary borrowing and using credit responsibly if they choose to do so.

8. Regularly Reviewing Expenses:

Periodically reviewing expenses aids in identifying spending patterns and areas where adjustments can be made. Encouraging teens to assess their spending habits allows them to make informed decisions about where to cut costs or reallocate funds.Inculcating these smart spending habits in teenagers equips them with lifelong skills for prudent financial management. These habits foster mindfulness, discipline, and a thoughtful approach to spending, setting the stage for a financially secure and responsible future.

Differentiating needs from wants

Differentiating between needs and wants is fundamental in cultivating responsible spending habits for teenagers. This distinction empowers them to prioritise essential expenditures, make informed financial decisions, and manage their resources effectively.

Understanding Needs:

Needs are necessities crucial for basic survival and well-being. They encompass fundamental expenses required to sustain a healthy and functional lifestyle. These typically include:

- **Food:** Essential for nourishment and sustenance.
- **Shelter:** Housing or accommodation providing safety and protection.

- **Clothing:** Basic attire suitable for weather and daily activities.
- **Education:** Access to learning resources and schooling.
- **Healthcare:** Medical care and wellness essentials.

Recognizing these needs as non-negotiable expenses is crucial. They form the foundation of a secure and healthy life, making them top priorities in budget allocation.

Differentiating Wants:

Wants, unlike needs, are desires or non-essential items that enhance comfort, entertainment, or personal enjoyment. These expenses are discretionary and are not imperative for survival. Some examples of wants include:

Entertainment: Non-essential activities such as dining out, movie tickets, or subscriptions to entertainment services.

Luxury Items: Items beyond basic necessities, such as high-end fashion, electronics, or accessories.

Travel And Recreation: Vacations, leisure activities, or hobby-related expenses.

Gadgets And Technology: Non-essential devices or upgrades not critical for daily functioning.Understanding the distinction between needs and wants allows teenagers to make conscious spending choices. It enables them to evaluate whether an expense is essential for their well-being or merely enhances their lifestyle or comfort.

Prioritising Needs Over Wants:

Recognizing needs as the primary focus of spending ensures that essential requirements are fulfilled before indulging in discretionary expenses. Prioritising needs over wants ensures financial stability and prevents overspending on non-essential items, contributing to responsible financial management.

Making Informed Decisions:
Teaching teenagers to differentiate between needs and wants fosters critical thinking about their spending habits. It enables them to assess the necessity and value of each expense, encouraging conscious decision-making aligned with their financial goals.

Budgeting And Allocations:
In budgeting, needs are allocated the highest priority and receive the largest share of financial resources. After fulfilling essential needs, teenagers can allocate funds towards wants if there's a surplus. This approach ensures that needs are met without compromising financial stability or accumulating debt.

Delayed Gratification And Long-Term Goals:

Understanding the distinction between needs and wants cultivates the habit of delayed gratification. Teens learn to prioritise long-term goals over immediate desires, recognizing that delaying certain wants can lead to more significant rewards or fulfilment in the future.

Differentiating needs from wants is pivotal in fostering financial literacy and discipline among teenagers. It empowers them to make informed choices, allocate resources sensibly, and cultivate a mindset of responsible spending that serves them well into adulthood. This understanding lays the groundwork for prudent financial management, enabling them to navigate their financial journey with foresight and purpose.

Making Informed Spending Decisions

Making informed spending decisions is a critical skill for teenagers, enabling them to manage their finances wisely, prioritise their needs, and work towards their financial goals. This process involves thoughtful consideration, research, and evaluation before making purchases or allocating funds.

Understanding The Value:
Before making a purchase, it's essential for teenagers to assess the value of the item or service they intend to buy. This evaluation involves considering factors such as quality, durability, functionality, and its contribution to their well-being or lifestyle. Understanding the value ensures that the expense aligns with their priorities and offers long-term benefits.

Research And Comparison:

Encouraging teenagers to research and compare options before making a purchase is crucial. Whether it's comparing prices, reading product reviews, or exploring different brands or alternatives, this practice helps in finding the best possible deal or value for their money. By being informed, they avoid overspending and ensure that they're getting the most out of their purchase.

Assessing Needs Vs. Wants:
Understanding the difference between needs and wants aids in making informed spending decisions. Teens should assess whether a purchase addresses a genuine need or fulfils a desire. Prioritising needs ensures that essential expenses are met before allocating resources to discretionary spending.

Budget Alignment:
Before making a purchase, teens should consider whether it fits within their budget. Aligning the expense with their budgetary

constraints ensures that they're not overspending or compromising other financial commitments. It promotes financial discipline and responsible spending within their means.

Considering Long-Term Impact:

Evaluating the long-term impact of a purchase aids in making informed decisions. Teens should consider if the expense contributes to their long-term goals or if it's a short-term gratification. Assessing whether the purchase supports their financial aspirations or adds value over time helps in avoiding impulse buys.

Avoiding Emotional Spending:

Encouraging teenagers to avoid emotional spending is crucial. Emotional impulses, influenced by marketing, peer pressure, or temporary desires, can lead to impulsive purchases that may not align with their actual needs or long-term goals. Teaching them to pause, reflect, and consider the necessity of the expense helps in making rational decisions.

Understanding True Cost:

Teens should understand the full cost of a purchase, including any hidden fees, maintenance costs, or additional expenses associated with owning or using the item. This comprehensive assessment helps in avoiding surprises and ensures they're prepared for any additional expenses related to the purchase.

Weighing Immediate vs. Future Benefits:

Considering both immediate and future benefits of a purchase aids in decision-making. Evaluating whether the short-term pleasure justifies the long-term impact on their financial well-being helps in prioritising expenses that contribute positively to their lives.

In essence, making informed spending decisions involves thoughtful consideration, research, and evaluation. Instilling this habit empowers teenagers to allocate their resources wisely, avoid unnecessary expenses, and ensure that their spending aligns with their priorities and financial goals. It equips them with the skills needed to make sound financial choices and build a solid foundation for responsible financial management in the future.

CHAPTER 5

Saving and Investing

Understanding the concepts of saving and investing is crucial for teenagers as they navigate their financial journey. Both practices involve setting aside money, but they serve different purposes and have distinct approaches.

Saving:

Saving involves setting aside a portion of income for short-term goals or unexpected expenses. It's a crucial habit that provides financial security and flexibility. For teenagers, saving can include:

Emergency Fund: Creating an emergency fund helps cover unexpected expenses like medical emergencies, car repairs, or sudden household needs without disrupting their budget or resorting to debt.

Short-Term Goals: Setting aside money for specific short-term goals, like purchasing a gadget, going on a trip, or buying gifts, encourages disciplined savings habits and fosters goal achievement.

Investing:

Investing, on the other hand, involves putting money into assets or ventures with the expectation of generating returns or increased value over time. Investing typically targets long-term financial growth and wealth accumulation. For teenagers, investing options may include:

Stocks and Bonds: Investing in stocks or bonds of companies or organisations allows teens to participate in the financial markets, potentially earning dividends or interest over time.

Mutual Funds or ETFs: Investing in mutual funds or exchange-traded funds (ETFs) provides diversification by pooling money with other investors, spreading risk, and potentially offering returns based on market performance.

Education Savings Accounts: Consideration of accounts like 529 plans, which offer tax advantages for education expenses, enables teens or their families to save specifically for educational purposes.

Differences and Benefits:
The key difference lies in their purposes and timelines. Saving focuses on preserving and accumulating funds for short-term goals or emergencies, while investing aims for long-term growth and potential wealth creation.

Risk And Returns: Saving typically involves lower risk as funds are often held in savings accounts or low-risk instruments, ensuring the safety of the principal amount. Investing involves varying degrees of risk, with the potential for higher returns but also the possibility of losses.

Time Horizon: Saving is short-term focused, usually for needs within a few months to a few years, while investing aims for long-term growth over years or decades.

Financial Goals: Saving is vital for immediate or near-future needs, while investing is geared towards achieving long-term financial goals like retirement savings, purchasing a home, or building wealth.

Balancing Saving And Investing:
Teaching teenagers the importance of striking a balance between saving and investing is crucial. While saving ensures financial security and addresses short-term needs, investing helps in wealth-building and achieving long-term financial goals.Encouraging teens to

start early, even with small amounts, allows them to harness the power of compounding and benefit from long-term growth.

Moreover, educating them about risk and diversification helps in making informed investment decisions aligned with their risk tolerance and goals.In summary, understanding the distinctions between saving and investing empowers teenagers to make informed choices about managing their money. Cultivating both habits equips them with the tools to achieve financial security, pursue their goals, and lay a strong foundation for a financially sound future.

Importance of saving money

Stability.

1. Financial Security:

Saving money creates a safety net, providing a cushion for unexpected expenses or emergencies. This financial buffer shields against sudden financial setbacks like medical emergencies, car repairs, or job loss, preventing individuals from falling into debt or financial turmoil.

2. Achieving Goals:

Saving is instrumental in achieving both short-term and long-term goals. Whether it's funding education, purchasing a car, travelling, or saving for a future home, setting aside money systematically allows individuals to realise their aspirations and turn them into tangible achievements.

3. Building Wealth:

Saving lays the groundwork for wealth-building. Even small amounts accumulated over time through consistent saving can grow significantly, especially when invested wisely. This habit harnesses the power of compounding, where saved funds generate returns that further contribute to financial growth.

4. Financial Independence:

Saving cultivates financial independence. By accumulating funds, individuals gain the freedom to make choices without relying on others or being constrained by financial limitations. This independence fosters confidence and autonomy in managing one's affairs.

5. Stress Reduction:

Having savings reduces financial stress. Knowing that there's a financial safety net alleviates anxiety related to unexpected expenses or uncertainty about the future. This sense of security contributes to overall well-being and peace of mind.

6. Opportunity For Investment:

Saving provides opportunities for investment. Accumulated savings can be channelled into investments that offer potential growth or generate passive income. This avenue enables individuals to explore options that contribute to long-term financial growth and wealth creation.

7. Preparation For Retirement:

Early saving habits pave the way for a comfortable retirement. Starting to save early allows for more time to accumulate funds, benefit from compounding returns, and build a robust retirement nest egg.

8.Developing Discipline And Responsibility:

Saving instils discipline and financial responsibility. It cultivates a habit of prioritising financial goals, making thoughtful spending decisions, and avoiding impulsive purchases. This habit of self-discipline translates into other aspects of life, fostering responsible decision-making.

9. Teaching The Value Of Money:

Saving teaches the value of money and the effort required to earn it. It promotes a deeper understanding of the significance of financial resources and encourages a mindset of thriftiness and mindful spending.

Encouraging teenagers to save early, even with modest amounts, kickstarts a journey towards financial empowerment. It equips them with invaluable skills, instils crucial habits, and sets the stage for a lifetime of financial prudence and security.In essence, the importance of saving money transcends the simple act of accumulating funds—it shapes financial habits, empowers individuals to achieve their aspirations, provides security in times of uncertainty, and establishes the foundation for a happy and prosperous future.

Introduction to basic investment concepts

Understanding basic investment concepts lays a crucial foundation for individuals venturing into the world of investing. These fundamental concepts elucidate the principles, risks, and strategies involved in making informed investment decisions.

1. Risk And Return:

Risk and return are intertwined in investing.In general, increased risk is correlated with better returns. Investments offering potentially greater returns often carry greater risk of loss. This concept highlights the importance of balancing risk tolerance with investment goals.

2. Diversification:

Diversification involves spreading investments across various asset classes, industries, or geographical regions to reduce risk. By not putting all eggs in one basket, diversification helps mitigate the impact of adverse events on the overall portfolio.

3. Asset Allocation:

Asset allocation refers to the distribution of investments across different asset classes like stocks, bonds, real estate, and cash equivalents. It plays a pivotal role in achieving investment goals while managing risk. Proper asset allocation aligns with an individual's risk tolerance, time horizon, and financial objectives.

4. Compounding:

Compounding refers to the process where the returns generated from an investment are reinvested, leading to exponential growth over time. This concept underscores the significance of starting to invest early to benefit from the power of compounding.

5. Investment Risk Types:

Understanding various types of investment risks—such as market risk, inflation risk, interest rate risk, and liquidity risk—helps individuals assess the potential challenges and volatility associated with different investments. Each risk type requires specific considerations in investment decisions.

6. Investment Vehicles:

Investment vehicles represent the different options available for investing, such as stocks, bonds, mutual funds, exchange-traded funds (ETFs), real estate, and commodities. Knowing the characteristics, risks, and potential returns of each investment vehicle assists in making informed choices.

7. Dollar-Cost Averaging:

Investing a set sum of money on a regular basis, regardless of market movements, is known as dollar-cost averaging.This strategy reduces the impact of market volatility and allows investors to buy more shares when prices are low and fewer when prices are high, potentially resulting in a lower average cost per share over time.

8. Investment Horizon:

Investment horizon refers to the duration an investor plans to hold an investment before needing the funds. It's a critical factor in determining the investment strategy, asset allocation, and risk tolerance. Longer investment horizons often allow for a more aggressive investment approach.

9. Inflation And Real Returns:

Recognizing the impact of inflation on investments is crucial. Investments should aim to outpace inflation to maintain purchasing power over time. Real returns, adjusted for inflation, provide a clearer understanding of an investment's actual growth in value.

Understanding these basic investment concepts forms a solid groundwork for individuals stepping into the investment landscape. It empowers them to make informed decisions, assess risks, align investments with their goals, and develop strategies that suit their financial objectives and risk tolerance. Continuously learning and applying these concepts enable individuals to navigate the complexities of investing with confidence and prudence.

CHAPTER 6

Dealing with Challenges

Dealing with challenges is an integral part of any financial journey, teaching individuals resilience, adaptability, and the ability to overcome obstacles. When faced with challenges in the realm of personal finance, several approaches can aid in navigating and mitigating these hurdles:

1. Financial Education:

Enhancing financial literacy equips individuals to tackle challenges with confidence. Continuous learning about budgeting, investing, debt management, and financial planning provides tools to navigate unforeseen circumstances.

2. Emergency Fund:

Building and maintaining an emergency fund acts as a safety net during unexpected financial setbacks. Having readily accessible funds helps in mitigating the impact of emergencies without disrupting long-term financial goals.

3. Adapting Financial Plans:

Flexibility in financial plans allows for adjustments in response to changing circumstances. Being open to modifying budgets, investment strategies, or savings goals ensures alignment with current needs and priorities.

4. Seeking Guidance:

Consulting financial advisors or mentors can yield insightful information.Consulting with professionals helps in developing strategies to address challenges, whether it's managing debt, planning for major expenses, or investing during market fluctuations.

5. Controlling Expenses:

During challenging times, controlling discretionary spending becomes essential.

Reevaluating expenses and identifying areas to cut back temporarily helps in redirecting funds towards more critical needs.

6. Long-Term Perspective:

Maintaining a long-term perspective fosters resilience. Recognizing that financial challenges are often temporary and that staying committed to financial goals can yield positive outcomes helps in staying focused during tough times.

7. Persistence and Patience:

Persistence and patience are key virtues. Overcoming financial challenges might require time and effort. Staying persistent in efforts to manage finances effectively and patiently working through difficulties leads to eventual success.

By adopting these approaches, individuals can navigate financial challenges with resilience, learn from setbacks, and emerge stronger and more adept at managing their finances. Embracing challenges as opportunities for growth and learning fosters a mindset of adaptability and preparedness in dealing with any financial adversity.

Overcoming common budgeting obstacles.

Overcoming common budgeting obstacles requires proactive strategies and a flexible mindset. Several challenges often hinder successful budgeting, but these obstacles can be addressed with the following approaches:

1. Overspending:

Overspending often derails budgeting efforts. Implementing a strict budget, tracking expenses meticulously, and practising conscious spending habits help in curbing overspending. Setting spending limits for different categories and regularly reviewing expenses aid in staying within budget.

2. Irregular Income:

Irregular income poses challenges in creating a consistent budget. Adopting a flexible budgeting approach by basing it on the lowest expected income, creating a buffer with extra earnings, and prioritising essential expenses ensures financial stability despite fluctuations.

3. Unexpected Expenses:

Unexpected expenses disrupt budget plans. Establishing an emergency fund specifically for unforeseen costs acts as a financial cushion. Allocating a portion of income towards this fund ensures readiness to tackle unexpected financial needs without affecting the core budget.

4. Debt Repayment:

Managing debt can be challenging within a budget. Prioritising debt repayment by allocating a dedicated portion of the budget to pay off debts gradually helps in reducing financial burden and freeing up funds for other expenses or savings.

5. Lifestyle Adjustments:

Lifestyle adjustments might be necessary to align with budgetary constraints. Identifying areas where spending can be reduced or making temporary sacrifices ensures that the budget remains realistic and sustainable.

6. Lack Of Discipline:

Lack of discipline in adhering to a budget hampers financial progress. Implementing strategies like automatic transfers to savings, avoiding impulse purchases, and periodically reviewing and adjusting the budget fosters discipline and accountability.

7. Unrealistic Expectations:

Setting realistic goals within the budget prevents disappointment and frustration. Establishing achievable milestones and acknowledging progress, even if gradual, encourages continued commitment to the budgeting process.

By acknowledging these common budgeting obstacles and applying tailored strategies, individuals can effectively overcome challenges, sustain their budgeting efforts, and achieve greater financial stability and control. Flexibility, discipline, and a proactive approach are key in successfully navigating these obstacles and maintaining a balanced financial plan.

Adapting and staying on track

Adapting and staying on track with a financial plan involves a dynamic approach that accommodates changes while maintaining focus on long-term goals. Several strategies facilitate adaptability and help individuals stay committed to their financial plans:

1. Flexibility In Budgeting:

Embracing flexibility in budgeting allows for adjustments in response to changing circumstances. Allocating funds according to evolving needs, revising spending categories, and accommodating unexpected expenses within the budget ensure adaptability without derailing financial goals.

2. Regular Review And Adjustment:
Regularly reviewing the financial plan aids in identifying areas that need modification. Analysing spending patterns, assessing progress towards goals, and making necessary adjustments ensure that the plan remains relevant and aligned with current needs.

3. Emergency Fund Maintenance:
Maintaining an emergency fund acts as a buffer against unexpected financial hurdles. Continuously funding and replenishing this reserve safeguards the budget from unforeseen expenses, enabling individuals to stay on track with their primary financial objectives.

4. Reassessment Of Financial Goals:

Reassessing financial goals periodically allows for realistic goal-setting. As circumstances change, priorities might shift, necessitating adjustments to align goals with current needs and aspirations.

5. Seeking Professional Guidance:

Seeking guidance from financial advisors or mentors assists in staying on track. Expert advice helps in navigating complex financial situations, making informed decisions, and ensuring that the financial plan remains on course.

6. Consistent Tracking Of Progress:

Consistently tracking progress towards financial goals provides motivation and accountability. Utilising tools or apps to monitor spending, savings, and investments helps in staying mindful of progress and staying motivated to adhere to the financial plan.

7. Flexibility In Investment Strategies:

Being flexible with investment strategies allows for adjustments based on market conditions or personal circumstances. Diversification, periodic portfolio rebalancing, and staying informed about investment options aid in adapting investment approaches without deviating from long-term objectives.

By embracing adaptability and employing these strategies, individuals can navigate changing financial landscapes, overcome obstacles, and ensure that their financial plans remain resilient, relevant, and aligned with their aspirations despite inevitable changes.

BOOK 2

CHAPTER 1

CAREER PLANNING

Understanding Yourself and Career Exploration

Understanding oneself is the first step towards embarking on a fulfilling career journey. This chapter delves into the significance of assessing interests, strengths, and exploring various career paths.

Assessing Interests And Strengths

Understanding one's interests and strengths is crucial. It involves introspection, self-assessment tools, and engaging activities to identify what truly captivates and motivates an individual. Interests often align with potential career paths, and recognizing these passions can significantly aid in choosing a suitable profession. Strength assessments, such as identifying key skills, talents, and personal qualities, play a pivotal role in guiding career choices. The chapter will delve into various assessment methods, exercises, and real-life examples to help teens better comprehend their unique traits and inclinations.

Exploring Diverse Career Paths

Once individuals have a clearer understanding of their interests and strengths, exploring diverse career paths becomes the next step. This section emphasises the importance of researching various professions, understanding their requirements, day-to-day responsibilities, growth opportunities, and alignment with personal values. Exposure to different industries through internships, shadowing experiences, or informational interviews can provide valuable insights into what a career entails.

It also discusses unconventional career paths and the evolving job landscape to encourage teens to consider new and emerging fields.This outline sets the stage for discussing the significance of self-assessment, exploring interests, strengths, and the importance of exposure to diverse career paths. Expanding on these points with real-world examples, exercises, and case studies can further enrich this chapter, providing valuable guidance to teens in their career exploration journey.

Assessing Interests and Strengths

Understanding oneself is the cornerstone of effective career planning. The process begins by delving into one's interests and strengths, a fundamental exploration that guides individuals toward professions that align with their passions and abilities.

Exploring Interests:

Identifying interests involves introspection and exploration. It's about pinpointing activities, subjects, or hobbies that ignite a sense of passion and enthusiasm. For a teen, this might involve reflecting on the subjects they enjoy studying, extracurricular activities they eagerly participate in, or causes they find themselves drawn to. It could also encompass their hobbies, be it art, technology, sports, or community involvement. Through self-assessment tools like career quizzes, interest inventories, or journaling exercises, teens can gain deeper insights into what truly captivates their attention and drives their curiosity.

Unearthing Strengths:

Strength assessment revolves around recognizing personal talents, skills, and qualities. It's about acknowledging what one excels at and where their natural inclinations lie. This might involve analysing academic achievements, identifying specific skills such as problem-solving, communication, leadership, or creativity, and acknowledging personal qualities like resilience, adaptability, or empathy. Tools such as strength assessments, feedback from mentors or teachers, or even peer discussions can aid in comprehending one's strengths more comprehensively. Recognizing these strengths not only boosts self-confidence but also helps in mapping out career paths that leverage these innate abilities.

Integration And Alignment:

The true power lies in the intersection of interests and strengths. When individuals recognize where their passions align with their natural talents, they uncover potential career paths that resonate deeply with them. For instance, someone passionate about environmental conservation and possessing strong analytical skills might find a fulfilling career in environmental science, data analysis for sustainability, or policy-making for eco-friendly initiatives. It's at this intersection that the most rewarding and fulfilling career choices often reside.

Utilising Assessment Tools:

There's a multitude of assessment tools available to aid teens in this process. These tools range from career quizzes to strengths-based assessments, each offering a structured way to delve deeper into one's interests and strengths. It's crucial to remind teens that these assessments are not definitive answers but rather guiding tools to prompt self-reflection and provide directional cues.

By engaging in this self-exploration journey, teens gain a clearer understanding of what truly motivates them and where their inherent capabilities lie. This clarity forms the bedrock for making informed career decisions, leading them toward paths that not only promise professional success but also personal fulfillment.Expanding on these points with relatable examples, case studies, and practical exercises can provide a comprehensive understanding of how teens can assess their interests and strengths to navigate their career paths.

Exploring Diverse Career Paths

Exploring diverse career paths is an essential step in a teenager's journey towards finding the right profession. This exploration phase goes beyond the surface, delving into the intricacies of various professions, their requirements, day-to-day realities, and future prospects.

Researching Professions:

Teens embarking on this exploration should engage in thorough research about different career options. This involves studying job descriptions, educational qualifications, and potential growth trajectories for various fields. Online resources, career guidebooks, informational interviews with professionals, and attending career fairs are effective ways to gather comprehensive information. Understanding the nuances of each profession helps in making informed decisions rather than relying on preconceived notions or stereotypes.

Alignment with Personal Values And Lifestyle:

Beyond the surface-level understanding of a profession, teens must assess whether a career aligns with their personal values and desired lifestyle. Some may prioritise stability and a structured work environment, while others might seek creativity and flexibility. Exploring how a particular career path fits into their long-term aspirations, personal values, and work-life balance preferences is crucial. For instance, a teen passionate about humanitarian causes might find satisfaction in careers like social work, non-profit management, or international relations.

Exposure And Experience:

Practical exposure significantly enriches the understanding of different careers. Internships, job shadowing, volunteer work, or part-time jobs in various fields provide firsthand experience, allowing teens to witness the day-to-day realities of a profession. Such experiences can confirm or redirect their career aspirations, offering invaluable insights that cannot be attained through mere research.

Adaptability And Evolving Job Market:
Encouraging adaptability is crucial in today's dynamic job market. Teens should understand that career paths might evolve, and embracing lifelong learning and adaptability is essential. Encouraging them to stay informed about emerging industries, technological advancements, and transferable skills prepares them to navigate future changes in their chosen career paths.

By immersing themselves in diverse career paths, teens gain a more profound understanding of various professions, allowing them to make informed decisions aligned with their interests, strengths, and aspirations for the future.

CHAPTER 2

Navigating Education and Skill Development

Navigating education and skill development is a pivotal aspect of a teenager's career planning journey. This chapter focuses on making informed choices regarding education, skill acquisition, and the significance of practical experiences.

Choosing Courses And Skill Enhancement:

Selecting the right courses plays a crucial role in shaping a teen's career path. It involves a thoughtful consideration of subjects that align with their interests and future aspirations. This section encourages teens to explore diverse subjects, emphasising not only academic relevance but also the development of critical thinking, problem-solving, and communication skills.

Additionally, it highlights the importance of extracurricular activities, workshops, or online courses that supplement formal education and enhance skill sets. For instance, a teenager interested in computer science might complement their academic coursework with coding classes or participation in hackathons.

Engaging In Internships And Networking:

Practical experiences gained through internships and networking are invaluable. This segment emphasises the significance of internships in providing hands-on exposure to a chosen field. It encourages teens to seek out internship opportunities, workshops, or mentorship programs that allow them to apply classroom knowledge in real-world scenarios. Networking is also highlighted as a crucial skill.

Building professional relationships, attending industry events, and connecting with professionals in their field of interest can open doors to future opportunities. This section provides guidance on how to approach networking, etiquette, and the benefits of mentorship.

Balancing Academics And Practical Skills:

A harmonious balance between academic pursuits and practical skill development is essential. While academic knowledge forms the foundation, practical skills and experiences often distinguish individuals in the job market. Encouraging teens to seek out projects, volunteer work, or part-time jobs relevant to their interests aids in skill development and provides a holistic understanding of their chosen field.

Continual Learning And Adaptability:

Highlighting the importance of lifelong learning and adaptability is crucial. Emphasising that education doesn't stop after formal schooling instils a mindset of continual growth. Encouraging the pursuit of new skills, staying updated with industry trends, and adapting to technological advancements prepares teens for the ever-evolving job market.By guiding teens on educational choices, skill development, and the significance of practical experiences, they're better equipped to build a strong foundation for their future careers.

Choosing Courses and Skill Enhancement

Selecting courses and enhancing skills form the bedrock of a teenager's academic and professional development. This phase involves strategic decision-making, considering not just academic requirements but also skill acquisition and personal growth.

Strategic Course Selection:

Choosing courses entails more than fulfilling academic obligations; it's about shaping a well-rounded educational journey aligned with one's career aspirations. Encouraging teens to explore a diverse array of subjects broadens their horizons, fosters critical thinking, and cultivates a range of skills. For instance, a student interested in environmental science might complement their core courses with electives in sustainability, policy-making, or data analysis to gain a holistic understanding of the field.

Skill Enhancement And Extracurricular Activities:

Beyond classroom learning, engaging in extracurricular activities enriches a student's skill set. Encouraging participation in clubs, sports, arts, or community service fosters teamwork, leadership, creativity, and time management skills. Additionally, promoting involvement in workshops, seminars, or online courses relevant to their interests aids in skill enhancement. For instance, a student interested in journalism might benefit from joining the school newspaper and attending writing workshops to refine their craft.

Adaptive Learning And Flexibility:

Highlighting the importance of adaptability and a growth mindset in choosing courses is crucial. Encouraging teens to remain flexible, open to exploring new subjects, and adapting their course selections based on evolving interests and career goals cultivates a mindset of continual growth. This mindset prepares them to embrace changes in career paths and industries, fostering resilience and adaptability.

Future Career Alignment:

Encouraging teens to map their course selections to their desired career paths fosters a clearer understanding of the skills and knowledge required in their chosen field. It's essential to emphasise that course selection is not just about grades but about acquiring relevant skills and knowledge applicable in future professions.

Highlighting the link between chosen courses and potential career trajectories helps teens make informed decisions regarding their academic journey.Guiding teens through strategic course selection and skill enhancement empowers them to craft an educational path that not only meets academic requirements but also nurtures their interests, honed their skills, and aligns with their future aspirations.

Engaging in Internships and Networking

Engaging in internships and networking presents invaluable opportunities for teenagers to gain practical experience, build professional relationships, and pave the way for future career success.

Internships:

Internships serve as bridges between classroom learning and real-world application. Encouraging teens to seek internships in their areas of interest exposes them to the daily operations of their chosen field. Whether it's a summer internship at a local company or a part-time internship during the school year, these experiences offer hands-on learning, allowing teens to apply theoretical knowledge and gain insights into the professional environment. Internships provide a platform to develop industry-specific skills, understand workplace dynamics, and even clarify career preferences by experiencing different roles within a field.

Networking:

Building a professional network is a skill that can significantly impact a teenager's future career prospects. Encouraging teens to attend industry-related events, join professional organisations, or connect with professionals in their field of interest through platforms like LinkedIn helps broaden their professional circle. Teaching networking etiquette, the art of initiating conversations, and maintaining professional relationships aids in fostering connections that could lead to mentorship opportunities, job referrals, or valuable insights into a particular industry. Networking not only opens doors to opportunities but also exposes teens to diverse perspectives and career paths.

Benefits Beyond Experience:

Internships and networking offer benefits beyond mere experience. They provide a glimpse into workplace culture, ethics, and the expectations of various industries. Through internships, teens gain exposure to different work environments, helping them understand what resonates with them professionally and culturally. Networking, on the other hand, exposes them to different career trajectories, allowing them to learn from others' experiences and gather insights that can shape their own career journeys.

Encouraging teens to actively seek internships and engage in purposeful networking early on sets the foundation for their future professional growth. These experiences not only enhance their resumes but also equip them with practical skills and a network of contacts essential for their career development.

CHAPTER 3

Preparing for the Job Market

Preparing for the job market involves equipping teenagers with the necessary tools, skills, and mindset to enter the professional world confidently. This phase focuses on honing essential job-seeking skills and cultivating a professional attitude.

Crafting Resumes And Cover Letters:

Assisting teens in crafting compelling resumes and cover letters is crucial. Educating them about the significance of a well-structured resume that highlights their skills, experiences, and achievements is key. Providing guidance on tailoring resumes for specific job applications and crafting personalised cover letters that express their motivation and suitability for a role helps set them apart from other applicants. Workshops or tutorials on resume writing and cover letter etiquette can be immensely beneficial.

Mastering Interview Skills:

Preparing teens for interviews is essential for their success in the job market. Teaching them how to research the company, anticipate common interview questions, and formulate articulate responses demonstrates the importance of preparation. Conducting mock interviews or role-playing scenarios helps build their confidence and sharpens their ability to communicate effectively, showcasing their skills and suitability for the role. Additionally, emphasising the significance of professional demeanour, attire, and punctuality during interviews instils a sense of professionalism.

Professional Etiquette And Work Readiness:

Instilling professional etiquette and work readiness in teenagers is critical. Educating them about workplace norms, communication etiquette, and the importance of teamwork, reliability, and adaptability in a professional setting prepares them for the expectations of the job market. Teaching them how to navigate workplace challenges, manage time effectively, and handle constructive feedback cultivates resilience and adaptability, essential traits in any work environment.

Continuous Learning And Adaptability:
Encouraging teens to embrace lifelong learning and adaptability is essential in preparing them for a dynamic job market. Stressing the importance of staying updated with industry trends, pursuing further education or certifications, and being open to acquiring new skills fosters a mindset of continual growth, ensuring they remain competitive and adaptable in an evolving job landscape.

Preparing teenagers for the job market involves not just technical skills but also a mindset and attitude conducive to success in the professional world. Equipping them with these essential tools empowers them to navigate the job market confidently and embark on their career journeys with readiness and enthusiasm.

Crafting Resumes and Cover Letters

Crafting resumes and cover letters is an art that teenagers must master as they prepare to enter the competitive job market. These documents serve as their first impression on potential employers, highlighting their skills, experiences, and suitability for a role.

Structuring Compelling Resumes:

A well-structured resume is a crucial tool in a teenager's job search arsenal. It should succinctly showcase their academic achievements, relevant experiences (such as internships, volunteer work, or part-time jobs), extracurricular activities, and any notable accomplishments. Encouraging teens to tailor their resumes for each job application by highlighting skills and experiences relevant to the specific role demonstrates their suitability and enthusiasm. Emphasising clarity, professionalism, and the use of action verbs to describe achievements adds impact to their resumes.

Personalised Cover Letters:

Cover letters provide an opportunity for teenagers to express their motivations, aspirations, and how their skills align with the job requirements. Educating them on the importance of crafting personalised cover letters that reflect genuine interest and understanding of the company and role is essential. Encouraging them to articulate their strengths, experiences, and how they can contribute to the organisation's goals helps create a compelling narrative. Tailoring cover letters to address specific company needs or referencing a shared value or project demonstrates dedication and interest in the role.

Showcasing Transferable Skills:

Highlighting transferable skills gained from academics, extracurricular activities, or part-time jobs can be advantageous. Skills such as communication, teamwork, problem-solving, leadership, and adaptability are valued by employers across various industries. Encouraging teens to showcase these skills through specific examples or achievements in their resumes and cover letters adds depth and demonstrates their readiness for the professional world.

Seeking Feedback And Revisions:

Teaching teens the importance of seeking feedback and revising their resumes and cover letters is crucial. Having peers, mentors, or career advisors review their documents for clarity, relevance, and grammar ensures they present themselves professionally and effectively.By guiding teenagers in crafting compelling resumes and cover letters, they can effectively showcase their qualifications and enthusiasm, increasing their chances of making a strong impression on potential employers. These documents serve as their gateway to securing opportunities in the job market.

Mastering Interview Skills

Mastering interview skills is essential for teenagers as they prepare to enter the workforce. Effective interview preparation enables them to confidently articulate their strengths, experiences, and suitability for a role while showcasing their professionalism.

Thorough Research And Preparation:
Encouraging teens to research the company, its values, mission, and recent achievements is crucial. Understanding the company's culture and the specific job role they're applying for allows them to tailor their responses

effectively. Moreover, preparing responses to common interview questions and practising with mock interviews helps build confidence and ensures they're ready to articulate their experiences and skills concisely.

Articulating Experiences And Skills:

Teaching teenagers how to articulate their experiences and skills in a structured manner is pivotal. Encouraging them to use the STAR (Situation, Task, Action, Result) technique helps frame their responses effectively, emphasising specific situations, their role, actions taken, and the outcomes achieved. Sharing relevant examples from academic projects, extracurricular activities, or previous experiences showcases their capabilities and suitability for the role.

Professional Demeanor And Communication:

Emphasising the significance of professional demeanour during interviews is crucial.

Encouraging teens to dress appropriately, maintain good posture, make eye contact, and exhibit positive body language instals confidence and professionalism. Additionally, honing their verbal communication skills, such as speaking clearly, listening attentively, and structuring responses coherently, ensures they effectively convey their ideas and experiences.

Handling Challenges And Asking Questions:

Preparing teens for handling challenging interview questions or hypothetical scenarios equips them to respond calmly and thoughtfully. Teaching them to remain composed, acknowledge their thought process, and provide logical answers showcases their problem-solving abilities. Furthermore, guiding them on asking thoughtful questions about the role, company culture, or future opportunities demonstrates their genuine interest and engagement in the interview process.

By coaching teenagers on mastering interview skills, they become better equipped to navigate the interview process confidently. These skills not only enhance their chances of securing employment but also prepare them for future professional interactions and opportunities.

CHAPTER 4

Making Informed Decisions and Future Growth

Making informed decisions and planning for future growth are vital components of a teenager's career planning journey. This phase involves thoughtful consideration, strategic thinking, and a proactive approach towards shaping their career trajectory.

Decision-Making Strategies:

Guiding teenagers in making informed decisions about their career paths is essential. Encouraging them to consider their interests, strengths, values, and aspirations when evaluating various career options helps align their choices with their personal goals. Teaching them to weigh the pros and cons of each option, considering potential growth opportunities, industry trends, and job market demand aids in making informed decisions.

Adaptability To Changes In The Job Market:

Highlighting the importance of adaptability in a dynamic job market is crucial. Encouraging teenagers to stay updated with industry trends, technological advancements, and evolving job requirements prepares them to pivot and adapt to changes in their chosen field. Emphasising the value of lifelong learning, acquiring new skills, and staying agile in response to market shifts ensures their relevance and competitiveness.

Lifelong Learning And Career Advancement Strategies:

Instilling a mindset of continual growth and learning is paramount. Encouraging teenagers to view their career as a journey of growth and development fosters a proactive approach towards career advancement. Guiding them to set short-term and long-term career goals, create action plans, and seek opportunities for skill enhancement or further education lays the groundwork for their professional growth.

Seeking Mentorship And Networking Opportunities:

Emphasising the value of mentorship and networking aids in their professional development. Encouraging teenagers to seek guidance from experienced professionals in their field of interest provides valuable insights, advice, and support. Furthermore, nurturing their professional networks through industry events, online platforms, or alumni associations broadens their opportunities for mentorship, collaboration, and future career prospects.

By empowering teenagers to make informed decisions, adapt to changes, foster a growth mindset, and build valuable networks, they're better equipped to navigate their career paths and pursue opportunities for continual advancement and success.

Decision-Making in Career Choices

Making decisions about one's career path is a significant step in a teenager's life. This process involves a thoughtful examination of their interests, values, strengths, and aspirations to ensure alignment with their future goals.

Self-Reflection And Assessment:

Encouraging teenagers to engage in self-reflection is crucial in making informed career choices. This involves exploring their interests, hobbies, and passions. Self-assessment tools, career quizzes, and personality tests can aid in understanding their strengths, values, and preferred work environments. These insights serve as a compass, guiding them towards career paths that resonate with their intrinsic motivations.

Researching And Exploring Options:

Teens benefit greatly from exploring diverse career options. Encouraging them to research various professions, understand job requirements, growth opportunities, and industry trends broadens their horizons. Exposure to different fields through internships, informational interviews, or job shadowing experiences allows them to gain firsthand insights, helping them make informed decisions based on real-world experiences.

Weighing Pros And Cons:

Teaching teenagers to weigh the pros and cons of different career paths is essential. Factors such as job stability, growth prospects, alignment with personal values, work-life balance, and potential challenges should be considered. This critical analysis helps them make decisions aligned with their long-term aspirations rather than short-term trends.

Seeking Guidance And Mentorship:

Encouraging teenagers to seek guidance from mentors, teachers, or career counsellors provides valuable insights and support. Mentors can offer advice, share experiences, and provide perspective, aiding in decision-making. Additionally, connecting with professionals in their desired field through networking opportunities or informational interviews can provide clarity and guidance in navigating career choices.

Flexibility And Adaptability:

Instilling the notion of flexibility and adaptability is crucial. Encouraging teenagers to remain open to exploring new opportunities, embracing change, and being resilient in the face of uncertainty fosters a mindset conducive to navigating diverse career paths.By guiding teenagers through a structured decision-making process, they can make informed career choices that align with their interests, values, and aspirations, setting the foundation for a fulfilling professional journey.

Continuous Learning for Career Advancement

Continuous learning is the cornerstone of career advancement in today's ever-evolving job market. Encouraging teenagers to embrace a mindset of lifelong learning fosters adaptability, growth, and a competitive edge in their careers.

Adopting A Growth Mindset:

Instilling a growth mindset in teenagers is pivotal. Emphasising that learning doesn't end with formal education encourages them to view challenges as opportunities for growth. Teaching them to embrace mistakes as learning experiences and to persistently seek knowledge and skill enhancement prepares them for continual advancement in their careers.

Staying Updated With Industry Trends:

Encouraging teenagers to stay informed about industry trends, technological advancements, and emerging skills required in their chosen fields is crucial. Following industry publications, attending webinars, and participating in professional development programs keeps them abreast of changes and equips them with relevant knowledge.

Pursuing Further Education And Certifications:

Guiding teenagers to consider further education, certifications, or specialised courses that complement their career goals is beneficial. This could involve pursuing higher education, obtaining industry-specific certifications, or enrolling in workshops tailored to their field of interest. Such initiatives not only deepen their expertise but also increase their marketability.

Developing Transferable Skills:

Emphasising the importance of acquiring transferable skills is essential. Skills like communication, problem-solving, adaptability, and leadership transcend specific roles and industries. Encouraging teenagers to focus on developing these skills enhances their versatility and readiness for various career opportunities.

Cultivating A Curiosity For Learning:
Fostering a curiosity for learning beyond immediate job requirements is invaluable. Encouraging reading, exploring diverse subjects, engaging in hobbies, or pursuing interests outside their field of study broadens their perspectives and nurtures creativity, critical thinking, and adaptability.

By cultivating a culture of continuous learning, teenagers can proactively shape their careers. Embracing a mindset that values ongoing education and skill enhancement ensures they remain competitive, adaptable, and well-prepared for the evolving demands of the job market.

CONCLUSION

How to Budget for Teens' is more than just a guide to managing money, it's a blueprint for building a solid foundation for future success. By mastering the principles of budgeting outlined in this book, teenagers gain the essential financial literacy skills needed to navigate the complexities of adulthood with confidence. However, financial well-being extends beyond budgeting; it intersects with career planning in profound ways. As you absorb the knowledge within these pages, it's crucial to recognize the symbiotic relationship between financial stability and career choices.

Strategic career planning involves more than just selecting a job; it's about aligning your passions, skills, and aspirations with opportunities that offer long-term fulfilment and financial security. Whether you're considering further education, vocational training, or entrepreneurial ventures, each decision contributes to your financial trajectory. By integrating budgeting practices with proactive career planning, you're not merely managing your money; you're investing in your future.

So, as you embark on this journey of financial empowerment and career exploration, remember that every choice you make today shapes the landscape of tomorrow. Embrace the principles outlined in this book, seize control of your finances, and chart a course towards a future filled with prosperity, purpose, and limitless possibilities.

www.ingramcontent.com/pod-product-compliance
Lightning Source LLC
Chambersburg PA
CBHW071049290526
45795CB00004B/1407